GUMBO
FROM HOW TO WOW
A GUIDE TO ONE OF THE WORLD'S GREATEST FOODS

FROM AUTHOR
Deanie Comeaux Bahan

Dedication

To my parents, Clifford and Elisa Comeaux.
Everything they did, including cooking, was
infused with love.

Acknowledgements

According to the dictionary, acknowledgement is
"expressing gratitude or appreciation for
something". In this case that would take another
whole book. So, trying to keep the list short . . .

Amy Covington gave me the title, her wit and her
wisdom. Casey Johnson of Roux Brands pushed
me to get it done, collaborated on the cover and
pulled it all together. My sister Neila Eckler again
proved to be a proof reader extraordinaire. My
friends Kitty LeBlanc, Vicki Fontana Williams,
Megan Casher and Georgia Plain were always
there making my life easier so I could
concentrate on Gumbo. My sister-in-law Jean
Comeaux was there for me at crunch time.

My own little family -- Remy, Susan, Michael,
Neila and Katie. They are a constant source of
joy, love, inspiration and pride.

And for Mark. *Tu me manques encore.*

"Give a man a fish, and you have fed him once. Teach him how to fish and you have fed him for a lifetime."

or

"We have lots of recipes but once you really learn to make gumbo, you won't need them."

This book is set up to teach you how to make gumbo your style. Please read the first sections before going to the recipes. These chapters will teach you everything you need to know to adapt the recipes to make them your own.

Gumbo from How to Wow
ISBN: 978-0-692-52795-5

Library of Congress Control Number: 201591647

Published by
Durand & Co., LLC
7840 Essen Cove Drive
Baton Rouge, LA 70809
www.perfectspoons.com
info@perfectspoons.com
Printed in China

Contents

First, a Little History

Gumbo is truly the great melting pot of cultures and cuisines. Its roots come from diverse peoples and converge in what must be the most multicultural dish in America. Which may explain, in part, why even though it was born in South Louisiana its fame and popularity have spread across the country. The other part of the explanation? It's just plain good!

We believe that the word gumbo may derive from the West African word kin-gombo which means okra or, perhaps, from the Choctaw Indian word kombo which was their word for what we now call filé. Filé is the herb made by grinding up dried sassafras leaves and is sometimes used to thicken gumbo.

Who contributed to gumbo? The Africans brought the okra, the Native Americans brought us filé. The Spanish contributed bell peppers and tomatoes, the Italians the garlic and the Germans added their sausages. The French brought the roux that starts most gumbos today and the bouillabaisse that might have been the original inspiration.

Is gumbo Creole or Cajun? Both Creole foods and people are native to the New Orleans area and are a blend of ethnicities and culture. The term Cajun originated from *Les Acadians*, the French inhabitants of the Acadian region of Canada who were forced to leave the area after it was conquered by Britain in the early 1700's. Many migrated to Louisiana where they settled along the bayous and swamplands west of New Orleans.

The differences between their cuisines has blurred over the years but in the past Creole food was considered "city food" and Cajun food was "country food." One easy way to tell the difference between Creole and Cajun gumbo? Tomatoes. Traditional Cajun gumbo never has them; Creole usually does. Also, the roux of the Cajun gumbo is usually a little darker and the gumbo is a little spicier.

Right or Wrong?

One of the best things about making gumbo is that there is no right or wrong way to do it. If there are four experienced cooks sitting at a table and someone mentions gumbo, you'll soon have them arguing about the best way to make it. And it's likely to be four different ways.

There are just about as many gumbo recipes as there are cooks. Most of us started out making it just like our mothers or fathers did and eventually added our own twists. Since we can't print the millions of recipes that exist, we are giving you the basics, the classics and ideas for a few add-ons to make it your own. Just remember that making gumbo is an improvisational thing!

Gumbo Spoons

Have you wondered what spoon to give to your guests when serving gumbo? According to Wikipedia, the gumbo and chowder spoon is a round bowl, 7" spoon and is larger than a bouillon or cream soup spoon. It's perfect for any chunky soup. And, for making sure that the shrimp don't land in your lap!

Making a Roux for Gumbo

Any flour and fat combination cooked together and used as a thickener is a roux (pronounced "roo"). Fats can include butter, bacon fat and vegetable oil. The difference between the roux used for gumbo and that used for chowder is in the color. A white, or blonde, roux is only cooked for 3 or 4 minutes. Just long enough to get rid of the raw flour taste. This white roux is the basis for all cream sauces, everything from béchamel to creamy mac and cheese.

The roux used for a gumbo is cooked a lot longer. The longer the roux is cooked, the darker it will get and the nuttier the taste will be. But, the longer you cook it, the less thickening power it will have. That's why most gumbo recipes add the thickening okra or filé.

Four Shades of Roux

In cooking text books they talk about the four shades of roux – white, blond, brown and dark brown. They all have the same ingredients and the only difference is in the cooking time. The white roux which is used for cream sauces should take about 4 minutes to cook; the brown and dark brown used for gumbo could take 25 or so minutes. A roux needs to be cooked slowly and stirred constantly. If it burns, it's trash. Nothing will ruin the taste of a dish as much as a burned roux.

The Ingredients

The choice of fat used for your roux is totally up to you. A roux for gumbo is usually made with vegetable or peanut oil. For cream sauce or chowder we usually use butter or rendered bacon fat. Some cooks prefer a combination of fats. The choice is yours but do remember while cooking that butter burns easily. You have to stir it constantly

The Measurements

A lot of recipes call for equal parts of fat and flour. If you read the fine print under that it often says "by weight." Try using ¾ cup of fat to 1 cup of flour or use 1 cup of fat to 1½ cups of flour. This should give you a good thick roux. Add a little less flour if you prefer to make a thinner roux.

There really is no such thing as making too much roux. If you're making gumbo, I hope you're making a big pot full. If there is any leftover it will freeze well. Not planning on making a lot of gumbo at one time? Freeze your extra roux. You can keep it in the refrigerator for up to a week or in your freezer for 6 months. Let it come to room temperature before adding it to your pot. The oil and flour will probably have separated; just stir it well to re-blend.

Roux Recipes

Traditional Roux
Some gumbos like seafood may need a thinner roux than others. Just use even parts oil and flour.

1 cup of vegetable oil or other fat
1 1/3 cup of flour.

Stir the oil and flour together over medium high heat until the mixture begins to bubble. Lower the heat and continue to stir. Now, how simple is that?

Seafood gumbo usually has a thinner roux. For that, try equal parts of flour and oil.

White Roux for Cream Sauce or Chowder

As a base for chowder the roux only needs to be cooked for 4 or 5 minutes. Just long enough so that you won't have the taste of raw flour. The traditional white roux uses butter for the fat.

Brown Roux for Gumbo

This is going to take a good bit longer depending on how brown you want your gumbo to be. Just remember that it has to be stirred constantly. A burned roux is the easiest way to ruin a gumbo.

Microwave Brown Roux

I am well aware that making a roux in the microwave sounds like heresy to traditionalists. I thought the same thing until I tried it. I found no difference in taste and what a time saver!

1 cup vegetable oil
1 cup flour

Mix the oil and flour well in a microwave safe glass bowl preferably with a handle. I always use my large 8-cup Pyrex measuring cup. Microwave on high for about 6 minutes. Stir the roux well at this point and then microwave for another 30 seconds to 1 minute. Watch it carefully as it browns and stop cooking when it gets to the right brown color. Be carefully with the bowl because the roux is very hot. At this point you can add your celery, onions and bell peppers and microwave for another 2 to 3 minutes. Then add garlic and parsley and cook for another minute or two.

Tip: All microwaves are different and adjustments to the timing may need to be made. Just keep an eye on the color of the roux.

One of the great things about the microwave roux is that it is almost impossible to burn and ruin it.

Oven Baked Dry Brown Roux

I'm not sure that we can really call this a roux because it has no fat. But it's easy; it's a great

calorie saver and it will last a long time in your refrigerator to be used whenever you need a thickener. Place 1 to 6 cups of flour into a big iron skillet or heavy dutch oven. Put this into a preheated 400° oven for 45 minutes to 1 hour stirring every 10 minutes until it is the shade of brown you want.

You can mix this cooked flour with water, whisking well, and add it to your gumbo or add it to your pot while you sauté your seasoning vegetables.

Instant Roux

The microwave has shortened the roux making time a lot but if you don't even have that much time try the roux in a jar or the roux mixes such as Kary's, Savoies, or Tony Chachere. Search the internet for ordering info if you can't find it at your grocer or check the Sources and Resources section of this book. If your recipe calls for 1 cup of flour, use 1 cup of the roux in a jar.

Roux making tips

Helpful
Hints

- If black specks appear in the roux, it has burned. Trash it and start over. It's just oil and flour and you'll get it right next time.

- Have your onions, celery and other seasons chopped and ready to add to the roux as soon as the color is as dark as you want it. This will bring down the temperature of the cooking roux and keep it from getting darker. But, don't forget to keep stirring because it is still cooking!

15

- If you make your roux ahead of time or refrigerate extra roux, you can pour some of the excess oil from the surface to save a few calories.

- When adding stock to a roux, whisk it in a little at a time to keep the roux from separating.

- Use a really heavy bottomed pot to cook your roux. It helps you avoid scorching it.

How to make Gumbo

You've already made your roux following the directions in the last chapter and it's perfect. A nice shade of brown with a kind of nutty scent.

The Seasoning Vegetables

If you hear a cook from South Louisiana mention the Trinity they're probably not talking religion. They're talking about the triumvirate of seasoning: onion, green bell pepper and celery. If they mention the Holy Trinity it also includes garlic. Chop your seasonings before you make your roux, even the day before. How much? Check the recipes if you're just starting out but I  usually chop until the onions make me cry. That always seems to be enough! Once your roux is the right color it's time to add the trinity to the pot. This will bring down the temperature of the roux. Cook them gently; you want them tender but not browned. Five or so minutes should do it because they'll get more cooking time later.

Now Let's Talk Okra

You either love it or you hate it or it looks so weird that you don't even want to try it. Unless you want a really thin gumbo you have to use either okra or filé (never both!) to thicken it. Usually it's okra. Use it in gumbo once to get over your okra fear and you'll probably use it forever after. I have to admit I'm not a big okra fan except in gumbo. And even then I like it cooked down to the point that I can barely see it. If you're thinking about the notorious okra slime, don't think about it. It disappears as the gumbo cooks.

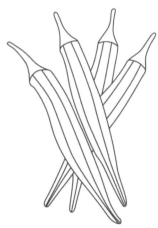

Fresh or frozen okra? That will pretty much depend on what's in season and where you live. If you can't get fresh, the frozen works well. When buying fresh okra try to get the smaller ones. They will be a lot more tender.

To prepare fresh or frozen whole okra wash it and dry it thoroughly. Cut off the tips and the hard ends and then slice it into ¼" rounds. Most of the frozen okra is already sliced; just throw away the hard end pieces. How much okra? Most recipes call for 1 to 2 pounds. When I have to use the frozen one I usually just throw in one full bag.

Decisions, Decisions

Now what? You've made your roux and cooked your onion, bell pepper and celery in it. Now it's decision time because there are a lot of different methods to adding the okra to the gumbo. I spoke to a good number of chefs and friends about when they add okra to their gumbos. As I suspected there were a lot of different methods.

I use the first method because I want my okra cooked down as much as possible and I don't want another pot to clean.

- Add the okra to the pot after you've sautéed your seasoning vegetables. Lower the heat so that you don't scorch the mixture. If it gets too thick (and it probably will) add a little water or stock. Let this cook for 10 or so minutes or until the okra is tender.

- A lot of recipes call for cooking the okra separately and then adding it to the gumbo. The only reason I know of for doing this would be to cook off some of the stickiness of the okra. I don't recommend doing this because that stickiness is what thickens the gumbo. It won't be sticky in your gumbo!

- During the summertime when fresh okra was plentiful, I remember my parents cooking a huge pot of it. They would sauté it with onions and a little bit of tomato. They would then divide it into freezer bags and freeze it so they would always have okra ready to go for wintertime gumbos. If your okra is pre-cooked you can put it into the pot when you add the stock.

- One good cook that I spoke to adds the raw chopped okra right after she adds the stock because she likes to bite down on a piece of okra. Another adds it during the last 5 to 10 minutes of

cooking time because he likes the
crunch of barely cooked okra.

- Several of my friends use no okra at all.
  Remember, no right or wrong with
  gumbo.

The Stock

A lot of gumbo recipes just call for water as the liquid. This will work if you have enough seasoning but using a chicken or seafood stock will always give you a richer, more flavorful gumbo. Stock is easy to make, can be made ahead of time and freezes well.

Seafood Stock

Don't throw away those shrimp heads and shells.  That's what you need to make the stock. If you don't have enough but you do have a friendly seafood market ask them to save shells and heads for you.

In a large pot put 4 quarts of water and about 2 pounds of shrimp heads and shells. Quarter 2 onions, 5 stalks of celery and 3 carrots and add them to the pot. Add 3 bay leaves, 3 cloves of garlic and salt and pepper to taste. Bring this to a boil, reduce the heat and let it simmer for an hour or two. Strain the broth and that's it! You've made homemade stock.

Chicken Stock

This is really simple; the recipe is the same as the Seafood Stock but you substitute chicken parts for the shrimp heads and shells.

After the Holiday Stock

Leftover turkey and tired of sandwiches? Make turkey and sausage gumbo. Use the stock recipe above and a pot big enough to hold the turkey carcass. When you strain the stock pick out any remaining turkey meat to add to the gumbo.

Ready Made Stock

Of course we know that homemade stock, whether it's seafood, chicken or beef, is usually better than store-bought. However, we also know that our time is often limited. Check your grocery store for Swanson's Cooking broths, Knorr Bouillon Cubes, Better Than Bouillon and the many other brands out there. They're good and will definitely yield a richer soup than water.

Gumbo Notes and Tips

- Making seafood gumbo? Don't add the shrimp or crabmeat until the last five or so minutes. Shrimp cook quickly and will get rubbery if cooked too long

- Adding sausage? Slice it and cook it separately for long enough to get most of the grease out before adding it to the gumbo. I often shorten my gumbo making time by cooking the chicken and the sausage in an oven safe pan at 350° for about 25 minutes. This way I can be making my roux and cooking my seasoning vegetables at the same time. You can also put the slices in the microwave to remove some of the grease.

- Gumbo can, of course, be eaten as soon as it's made. But it will always taste better the next day after the flavors have had time to blend.

- If you refrigerate the gumbo after you make it you'll be able to easily skim off any grease that has solidified on top.

- Time crunch? You can stop almost anywhere during the gumbo making process. Just refrigerate it and come back and finish it the next day.

- File' (pronounced fee-lay) is ground sassafras and is often used to finish off  gumbo. The early Cajuns learned about file' from the Choctaw Indians. Use either okra or filé as your thickener. Not both. And, never ever add filé to the pot and cook it. You'll have a stringy mess if you do.

- Tomatoes? Creoles and Cajuns are not the same people. Neither is their gumbo. Creole gumbo originated in the New Orleans area and often contains tomato. Cajun gumbo comes from the Acadians who settled South Louisiana outside of the New Orleans area and usually does not have tomato in it. In recent years there has been a big  crossover in the two styles of cooking so the choice is yours. If you do want to add tomato, don't add too much – this is not tomato soup! The canned peeled tomatoes work well.

- Gumbo is traditionally served over rice. The rice goes into the bowl and then the gumbo is ladled over it. Never add the rice to the pot! Some people like a small spoon of rice and some like a bowl full of rice and use the gumbo almost as a gravy.

- Gumbo is usually made with two or more varieties of meat or seafood – shrimp, crab, crawfish, oysters, smoked sausage, chicken, duck, turkey, etc. The choice is yours.

- Shhh – don't repeat this, but if you're finished cooking your gumbo and wish it were a little darker, run to your grocery store for Kitchen Bouquet and add it to your gumbo a few drops at a time until the gumbo is the perfect color. Kitchen Bouquet. Is one of those chef's helpers that has really stood the test of time. It was featured in the United States exhibit at the Paris Exposition of 1889!

- A lot of recipes call for Creole or Cajun seasoning mix. Check your grocer for Tony Chachere's, Zatarain's or even McCormick. Or make your own from the recipes in the Lagniappe section of this book.

- Andouille is a staple of many Creole and Cajun gumbos. It's a spicy, heavily smoked, coarsely ground pork sausage. If you can't find it locally you can order it online or substitute a good smoked sausage.

Recipes

This next section contains a lot of gumbo recipes from across the country. Some are Cajun or Creole style; some are definitely not. However, they're all good.

You may look at some of these recipes and say Huh? Gumbo with roasted potatoes in it? Black eyed peas? Red beans? Canned cream of chicken soup?

If you read the first part of this book, you've got your gumbo basics down. These non-traditional ingredients sound good? Put them in. Not so good? Leave them out. Do experiment so you can come up with your own signature style gumbo.

"There are thousands of gumbo cooks in the Gulf Coast area which means there are thousands of ways of making gumbo and no two pots are ever just alike."

Amy Covington
Bay St. Louis, MS

Simple Chicken and Sausage Gumbo

This is perhaps the simplest of the gumbos, but one that has become really popular because of the high cost of seafood. This recipe uses filé instead of okra as a thickener. Pass the filé at the table; do not add it to the pot.

If you decide to add okra don't use the filé. If you can't find andouille, any good smoked sausage will do.

- 1 cup oil
- 1 1/3 cup flour
- 2 large onions, chopped
- 2 bell peppers, chopped
- 4 ribs celery, chopped
- 4 cloves garlic, minced
- 4 quarts chicken stock
- 2 bay leaves
- 2 teaspoons Cajun Seasoning* or to taste
- Salt and pepper to taste
- Meat from 1 large chicken, cut into pieces
- 2 pounds andouille or smoked sausage, sliced
- 1 bunch green onions, tops only, chopped
- Cooked rice
- Filé powder to taste

*See the Lagniappe section for Creole and Cajun Seasoning recipes.

In a skillet brown the sausage and the chicken and pour off the excess fat.

In a large heavy pot make your roux by blending the oil and flour. Cook, stirring constantly, until you reach a deep brown color. This should take about 25 minutes.

Add the seasoning vegetables and continue to cook while stirring. It should take about 4 minutes to get the veggies to where they are wilted but not brown. About half way through the minutes add the garlic and lower the heat a little. Garlic burns easily.

Add the stock, seasonings, chicken and sausage. Bring to a boil and lower the heat to a simmer. Cook for about an hour.

Add the chopped green onion tops during the last 10 minutes. Serve over rice and pass the filé powder.

This makes about 12 meal size servings.

See the Lagniappe section of this book for Cajun Seasoning recipes and Sources and Resources for ordering info.

Seafood Gumbo

1-1/2 cup flour
1 cup vegetable oil
3 quarts stock (see page 22)
2 medium onions, chopped
1 cup chopped celery
1 large green bell pepper, chopped
4 cloves fresh garlic finely diced
1 tablespoon Cajun seasoning or to taste*
3 bay leaves
3 pounds medium shrimp, peeled
1 pound crabmeat, shells picked out
1/4 cup parsley, chopped
1 bunch green onions chopped
Filé, served at table**
Cooked rice to be served with gumbo

* See Lagniappe section for seasoning recipes

** If you choose to use okra instead of filé,
   find directions on page 18 .

In a large heavy pot make your roux by blending
the oil and flour. Cook, stirring constantly, until
you reach a nice caramel color. This should take
about 20 minutes. Add the chopped vegetables
and cook on medium heat for 5 minutes.

Add the stock to the pot slowly while stirring.
Add the Cajun seasoning and bay leaves. Let this
simmer for at least 1 hour.

Add the shrimp and crab meat and cook 5 minutes stirring gently a few times. Remove from heat, add green onions and parsley. Stir, cover and allow to sit for 15 minutes. Serve over rice.

Makes 10 meal size servings.

Notes:

_____

_____

_____

_____

_____

_____

_____

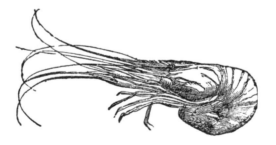

Creole Seafood Gumbo

1/4 cup oil
4 tablespoons flour
2 medium onions, chopped
2 stalks celery, chopped
1 bag frozen chopped okra
3 cloves garlic, minced
2 quarts chicken stock
1 - 16 ounce can diced tomatoes
2 bay leaves
Creole seasoning to taste
Salt & pepper to taste
Hot pepper sauce - optional
2 pounds raw shrimp, peeled
1 pound crabmeat
1 pint oysters

In a large heavy pot make your roux by blending the oil and flour. Cook, stirring constantly, until you reach a nice dark caramel color. This should take about 20-25 minutes. Add the chopped vegetables and cook on medium heat for 5 minutes. Add the okra and cook another 10 minutes.

Add stock, tomatoes, bay leaves, Creole seasoning and salt and pepper and simmer for 2 hours.

10 minutes before serving, add the raw seafood. Simmer 5-6 minutes. Serve in a soup bowl over rice.

Serves 6.

Shrimp and Crab Gumbo

1/2 cup oil
3/4 cup flour
1 large onion, chopped
1 bell pepper, chopped
3 ribs celery, chopped
4 cloves garlic, minced
1 pound okra, trimmed and sliced
1 gallon shrimp stock*
1 teaspoon thyme
Salt, freshly ground black pepper and cayenne
   pepper to taste
3 pounds medium shrimp, peeled
2 pounds fresh lump crabmeat, with shell bits
   picked out
6 cups cooked white rice
*See page 22 for Shrimp Stock directions

Mix the oil and flour in a large heavy pot blend well to start your roux. Cook the roux, stirring constantly, for about 25 minutes on medium heat until it is a rich caramel color.

Add the vegetable seasonings and cook while stirring for about 5 minutes. When the seasonings are tender add the okra and cook, stirring, for another 15 minutes.

Add the stock, salt, and pepper. Stir well and simmer over low heat for one hour.

Add the shrimp about 5 minutes before serving time and then add the crabmeat. Cook over gentle heat until the shrimp turn pink.

Serve in large soup bowls over 1/2 cup of cooked rice.

Makes 10-12 meal size servings.

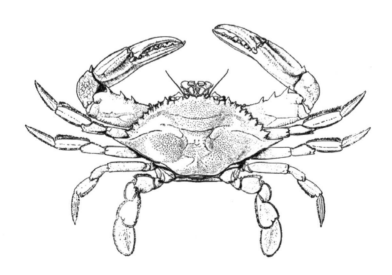

After Thanksgiving Turkey Gumbo

6 quarts of turkey stock made from leftover
   turkey carcass
1 1/3 cup flour
1 cup oil
2 onions, chopped
2 bell peppers, chopped
5 ribs celery, chopped
5 cloves garlic, minced
Leftover turkey meat, cut into bite-sized pieces
1 pound andouille or other smoked sausage,
   sliced
1 pound sliced okra
3 bay leaves
Cajun Seasoning or salt and pepper*
Salt and freshly ground black pepper, to taste
Tabasco Sauce (optional)
1 bunch fresh parsley, chopped
1 bunch chopped green onions tops
*See Lagniappe section of this book

Mix the oil and flour in a large heavy pot. Blend
well and cook the roux, stirring constantly, for
about 25 minutes on medium heat until it is a
rich deep caramel color.

When the roux reaches the right color add your
seasoning veggies. Cook while stirring for about
5 minutes. Lower the heat and add the garlic.

In a separate pan, brown the andouille or smoked sausage and pour off the excess fat.

Add the turkey stock to the roux and veggies slowly while stirring. Also add the sausage, turkey, okra, bay leaves and Cajun seasoning,

Bring to a boil and then reduce to medium heat and simmer for an hour.

Taste to adjust salt and pepper and add Tabasco if desired.

Serve over hot white rice.

Serves 12 with great leftovers.

Notes:

_____

_____

_____

_____

_____

_____

_____

Spicy Gumbo

1 1/2 cups of flour
1 cup vegetable oil
2 cups chopped onions
1 cup chopped green bell pepper
1 cup chopped celery
3 cloves of garlic, minced
3 quarts chicken stock
2-10 ounce cans Ro*Tel tomatoes
5 boneless chicken breast or 8 thighs cut into
   bite size pieces
3 cups andouille or other smoked sausage,
   chopped
1 bag frozen cut okra
1/3 cup chopped parsley
1 teaspoon Tabasco, optional
Salt and cayenne pepper to taste
Creole or Cajun seasoning to taste
3 bay leaves
1/4 cup chopped green onion

Mix the oil and flour in a large heavy pot and
blend well to start your roux. Cook the roux,
stirring constantly, for about 25 minutes on
medium heat until it is a rich deep caramel color.

Add onions, bell pepper, celery and garlic. Sauté
for 5-6 minutes until vegetables are soft but not
brown. Add stock, tomatoes, chicken, sausage,
okra, parsley, other seasonings and bay leaves.
Simmer for two hours. Add the green onion

during the last 20 minutes. Serve over rice to 10 hungry people.

Crawfish and Sausage Gumbo

1/2 cup oil
1/2 cup all-purpose flour
1 large onion, chopped
1 green bell pepper, chopped
2 stalks of celery, chopped
3 cloves of garlic, minced
1 pound frozen or fresh okra, sliced
2 quarts chicken broth
1 pound andouille or other smoked sausage, sliced
1/2 teaspoon thyme
3 bay leaves
2 teaspoons Tabasco sauce, optional
2 tablespoons Creole seasoning mix
Salt and pepper to taste
1 pound crawfish tails
4 cups of cooked white rice

Mix the oil and flour in a large heavy pot and  blend well to start your roux. Cook the roux, stirring constantly, for about 25 minutes on medium heat until it is a rich deep caramel color.

Add onions, bell pepper, celery and garlic. Saute' for 5-6 minutes until vegetables are soft but not brown. Add the okra and sauté for another 10 minutes. If the mixture gets too thick add some of the stock to the pot.

In a separate pan, brown the sausage and discard excess grease.

Add the stock slowly to the pot while stirring. Add the sausage, bay leaves and all of the seasonings. Simmer for 1 to 2 hours. Add the crawfish to the pot for the last 10 minutes of cooking time.

Season to taste with salt, black pepper, and cayenne pepper. Remove bay leaves.

Serve in a soup bowl over white rice.

Makes 6-8 servings.

Notes:

_____

_____

_____

_____

_____

_____

Simple Fast Gumbo

*Making a traditional gumbo takes a lot of time --
Time that we often don't have. This recipe takes a
lot of shortcuts and it's good!*

Roux in a Jar or Instant powdered roux
3 quarts canned chicken stock
2 cups pre-chopped onion and bell pepper
1 pound andouille or other smoked sausage,
   Sliced and cooked to remove grease
2 ½ cups of leftover rotisserie chicken
1/2 teaspoon black pepper
1 teaspoon Cajun or Creole seasoning
1/8 teaspoon Cayenne pepper
Salt to taste
2 bay leaves
1 teaspoon Tabasco Sauce or to taste

Helpful Hints

*If you can't find roux in a jar
at your local grocers check
Sources and Resources on
page 75.*

In a large pot, bring the stock to a boil. Follow the
directions on your quick roux package to
determine how much you will need. Add the roux
a bit at a time while stirring. When the stock and
roux are well blended add the seasoning
vegetables, sausage, chicken, seasonings and bay
leaves. Let this simmer for one hour.

Taste for salt and add Tabasco if you wish. If the gumbo is too thin, add some more of the roux.

Cook for another ½ hour. Serve to 8 hungry people over white rice.

Simple Fast Shrimp Gumbo

The ingredients and directions for this gumbo are almost identical to the Simple Fast Chicken and Sausage Gumbo.

Substitute shrimp for the chicken. Go ahead and use frozen shrimp if you really don't have time to peel fresh ones.

Do not add your shrimp until the last 10 minutes of cooking time.

Serve and enjoy!

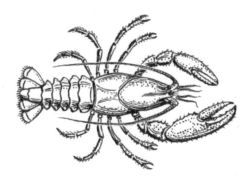

Crock Pot Gumbo

1/3 cup all-purpose flour
1/3 cup cooking oil
4 cups water
12 ounces smoked sausage, sliced
1 1/2 cups chopped cooked chicken
2 cups fresh okra or 1 package frozen, sliced
1 cup chopped onion
1/2 cup chopped green bell pepper
1/2 cup chopped celery
4 garlic cloves, minced
1/2 teaspoon each salt and pepper
1/4 teaspoon ground red pepper
1 (14 ounce) can diced tomatoes with liquid
1 (12 ounce) package frozen peeled shrimp

Make the roux in a heavy skillet. Stir together the flour and oil until smooth and then cook on medium high heat stirring constantly.
Cook over medium-high heat for 20 minutes or until the roux reaches a rich, dark caramel color.

Pour the water into the slow cooker and then stir in the roux and blend well. Wipe out your skillet and brown the sausage, pour out the excess grease and add the sausage to the crock pot along with all other ingredients except the shrimp. Cook on low heat for 6 ½ hours. Add the shrimp for the last 20 minutes cooking time.

Serve over white rice to 6 people.

Oyster Gumbo

1/2 cup oil
3/4 cup flour
2 medium onions, chopped
2 cups green bell pepper, chopped
1 cup celery, chopped
2 cloves garlic, minced
1 gallon shrimp stock
2 teaspoons salt
1 teaspoon freshly ground black pepper
1/4 teaspoon cayenne pepper or to taste
2 bay leaves
1/2 cup fresh parsley, chopped
1 pound medium shrimp, peeled
3 pints raw fresh oysters, with their liquor
Filé powder to taste
6 cups cooked long-grain white rice

In a large heavy pot combine the flour and oil to make your roux. Cook on a medium high heat, stirring constantly, until it reaches a deep brown color. Add the onion, bell pepper, celery and garlic. Cook, stirring constantly, until vegetables are tender but not browned.

Add the stock, seasonings, bay leaves and parsley. Bring the mixture to a boil and then lower the heat and simmer for 1 hour.

Five minutes before the cooking time is over add the shrimp, oysters and oyster liquor. Cook just until the shrimp turn pink, about 5 minutes.

Serve over cooked rice in a large soup bowls. Sprinkle a little filé powder in each bowl or pass it around at the table.

Serves 12.

Notes:

_____

_____

_____

_____

_____

_____

_____

Catfish Gumbo

1 stick butter
5 tablespoons flour
1 medium onion, chopped
1 medium bell pepper, chopped
2 stalks celery, chopped
1 pound okra, sliced
6 cups seafood stock
1 can diced tomatoes
1-1/2 teaspoon Cajun seasoning
1/2 teaspoon thyme
2 ounce smoked sausage or other meat, diced
    and browned
2 pounds catfish fillets in bite size chunks
1/3 cup parsley
Tabasco sauce to taste

In a large heavy pot melt the butter on medium heat and stir in the flour. Cook, stirring constantly, until the roux is caramel color. Be careful not to burn the butter. You don't need a very dark roux.

Add chopped vegetables and cook until soft stirring often. Put the okra in the pot and stir well. Cook this for about 10 minutes. If it gets too thick, add a little of the stock to thin it out.

Add the stock, tomatoes, seasonings and meat. Stir and simmer for an hour and a half. Add the parsley and fish and stir gently. Try not to break up the fish chunks. Simmer another half hour.

Serve over white rice. Serves 6-8.

Gumbo Z'Herbes, Gumbo Vert And Green Gumbo

These are all the same gumbo, just different names. It is a meatless gumbo that has been a traditional Lenten dish in South Louisiana for many years. Green Gumbo can include whatever mix of leafy green veggies you choose. During the rest of the year ham or other meats are often added.

¼ cup oil
¼ cup flour
2 large yellow onions, chopped
1 green bell pepper, chopped
3 stalks celery, chopped
4 cloves garlic, minced
8 cups of water
3 pounds of mixed greens like mustard, kale,
    spinach, parsley, etc. cleaned and chopped
2 teaspoon Tabasco sauce or to taste
Salt and pepper to taste
2 bay leaves
Cajun seasoning mix to taste
Filé powder

In a large heavy pot combine the flour and oil to make your roux. Cook on a medium high heat, stirring constantly, until it reaches a caramel color. Add the onion, bell pepper, celery and garlic. Cook, stirring constantly, until vegetables are tender but not browned.

Pour the water in and stir well to blend. Bring this to a boil and then add the greens and seasonings and bring to a boil. Add the bay leaves and reduce the heat. Simmer for 1 hour or until the greens are very tender.

Serve over white rice and pass the filé at the table.

Serves 10-12.

Notes:

_____

_____

_____

Venison Gumbo

1 cup oil, lard or bacon fat
1 1/4 cups flour
1 large green bell pepper, chopped
2 medium onions chopped
4 celery stalks, chopped
5 cloves garlic, minced
Salt, cayenne and black pepper to taste
2 tablespoons paprika
1 tablespoon dried thyme
1 tablespoon dried oregano
2 tablespoons garlic powder
1 teaspoon celery seed
3 quarts game stock, chicken stock or water
1 pound smoked andouille sausage, sliced and
    cooked to remove grease
4 pounds of venison, cubed
5 green onions, chopped
1/2 cup chopped parsley
Filé

Mix the oil and flour in a large heavy pot and
blend well to start your roux. Cook the roux,
stirring constantly, for about 25 minutes on
medium heat until it is a rich deep brown color.

Add onions, bell pepper, celery and garlic. Sauté
for 5-6 minutes until vegetables are soft but not
browned.

Pour the stock into the soup pot slowly while stirring. Add all of the dry spices except the filé and stir well.

Add the sausage and the venison and turn the heat up to high. When the gumbo starts to boil, turn the heat down and let it simmer, covered for about 3 hours. Stir occasionally and check the venison to see if it is cooked and tender. Tough venison may need to be cooked a little longer.

Put the green onions into the pot during the last 5 minutes of cooking time. Serve over white rice and pass the filé at the table.

Serves 8-12.

Notes:

_____

_____

_____

_____

_____

_____

Spicy Crawfish Gumbo

1 cup flour
3/4 cup oil
2 medium onions, chopped
2 stalks of celery, chopped
1 large green bell pepper, chopped
3 cloves garlic, minced
1 cup diced andouille or other smoked sausage
2 quarts chicken stock
1 10 ounce can Ro*Tel tomatoes
2 bay leaves
1 3/4 teaspoon Cajun seasoning
2 tablespoons chopped parsley
2 pounds of peeled crawfish tails
1/2 cup chopped green onions
File' powder

In a large heavy pot combine the flour and oil to make your roux. Cook on a medium high heat, stirring constantly until it reaches a deep brown color, about 25 minutes. Add the onion, bell pepper, celery and garlic. Cook, stirring constantly for about 5-6 minutes.

Brown the sausage in a skillet, the oven or the microwave and discard the excess grease.

Add the stock, sausage, Ro*Tel tomatoes, bay leaves and seasonings to the big pot. Simmer on low heat for 1 hour stirring occasionally.
Add crawfish tails, chopped parsley and green onions and simmer for another 20 minutes.

Serve over white rice and pass the filé at the table. Serves 10.

Notes:

_____

_____

_____

_____

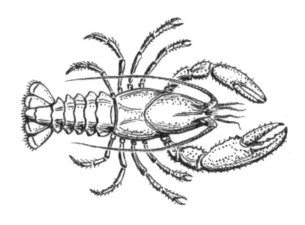

Chicken and Andouille Gumbo

Not crazy about okra or filé? That's okay. Here's one for you.

2 cups flour
1-3/4 cups oil
2 medium onions, chopped
1 medium bell pepper, chopped
3 stalks of celery, chopped
3 cloves of garlic, minced
3 quarts chicken stock
6 chicken breasts, torn into bite size pieces
3 cups andouille or other smoked sausage, sliced and browned
1 teaspoon Cajun seasoning
1 teaspoon Tabasco, optional
3 bay leaves
3 tablespoons chopped parsley
1/4 cup chopped green onion

In a large heavy pot combine the flour and oil to make your roux. Cook on a medium high heat, stirring constantly, until it reaches a deep brown color, about 25 minutes. Add the onion, bell pepper, and celery. Cook, stirring constantly for about 5-6 minutes. Stir in the garlic in the last couple of minutes. It burns easily.

Add the stock, chicken, sausage, seasoning, Tabasco and bay leaves. Simmer 1-2 hours. Add parsley for the last 20 minutes and green onion for the last 10. Taste to adjust seasoning and serve over white rice.

Serves 12 hungry people.

Easy Chicken and Shrimp Gumbo-laya

This is definitely not a traditional gumbo – no roux, okra or filé. But, it's both easy and good. You can substitute almost any leftover veggie you have in the refrigerator for the broccoli. Gumbo-laya is a cross between gumbo and jambalaya.

2 whole boneless chicken breasts, cut or pulled
  into bite size pieces
1/2 pound frozen peeled shrimp
4 cups water
1 can cream of chicken soup
1/2 can diced tomatoes with juice
1 small onion, chopped
1 celery stalk, chopped
1 bay leaf
1/2 cup raw broccoli
1 teaspoon Cajun seasoning
Cayenne pepper to taste
Salt to taste
1 teaspoon Worcestershire sauce
Tabasco to taste

Put all of the ingredients except the shrimp into a large soup pot. Start the cooking on high until it starts to boil. Lower the heat and allow to simmer for 1 hour. Add the shrimp in the last 10 minutes of cooking time. Serve over white rice.

Serves 6-8.

Black-Eyed Pea Gumbo

2/3 cup vegetable oil
2/3 cup flour
1 large onion, chopped
1 bell pepper, chopped
3/4 cup celery, chopped
3 cloves garlic, minced
1 pound okra, sliced
1 pound cooked ham, cubed
2 cans diced tomato
Salt and pepper, or to taste
8 cups water
1/3 cup parsley, chopped
2 bay leaves
2 cans black eyed peas

In a large heavy pot combine the flour and oil to make your roux. Cook on a medium high heat, stirring constantly, until it reaches a deep brown color, about 25 minutes. Add the onion, bell pepper, and celery. Cook, stirring constantly for about 5-6 minutes. Stir in the garlic in the last couple of minutes. It burns easily.

When the veggies are tender add the okra and sauté for another 15 minutes. If it gets too thick, add a little water. Stir often so the bottom doesn't scorch.

Add all of the remaining ingredients stirring well. Simmer for 45 minutes. Serve over white rice.

Serves 8.

Notes:

_____

_____

_____

_____

_____

_____

_____

Chicken and Sausage Gumbo with Roasted Potatoes

This is a pretty traditional gumbo until you get to the roasted potatoes. Gumbo is often served with potato salad in New Orleans but roasted potatoes are definitely unusual – and delicious.

1 pound andouille sausage or other smoked
  sausage, sliced
1/2 cup oil
3/4 cup flour
1 large onion, chopped
1 bell pepper, chopped
2 stalks celery, chopped
2 garlic cloves, minced
6 cups chicken broth
2 teaspoons Cajun seasoning or to taste
Pepper and salt to taste
2 pounds shredded chicken
Roasted Potatoes

In a large skillet cook the sausage until it is browned. You can also do this in the oven or microwave. Drain the excess grease and set the sausage aside.

In a large heavy pot combine the flour and oil to make your roux. Cook on a medium high heat, stirring constantly, until it reaches a deep brown color, about 25 minutes. Add the onion, bell pepper, and celery. Cook, stirring constantly for about 5-6 minutes. Stir in the garlic in the last couple of minutes. It burns easily.

Pour the chicken broth into the pot slowly while stirring to blend with the roux.

Add the sausage, chickens and seasonings. Bring this to a boil and then lower the heat and simmer for an hour and a half.

Put roasted potatoes in the bottom of each soup bowl and ladle the gumbo over.

Serves 6 – 8.

Roasted Potatoes

While your gumbo is simmering, preheat the oven to 425°. Wash and then cube the potatoes – small red, Yukon Gold, etc. Toss the potato chunks in a bowl with olive oil, salt and pepper.

Spread the potatoes on a baking sheet in a single layer. Bake for 40 minutes until the potatoes are fork tender. About midway through the cooking time, turn the potatoes so they'll brown evenly.

Lagniappe

This section contains recipes for seasoning mixes, soups and desserts that are not gumbo but are mighty good!

In South Louisiana lagniappe simply means "a little extra." It is pronounce "lan yap". Like the word gumbo, the word lagniappe has an interesting history. The Spanish brought the word *yapay* from the Incas to Louisiana. They spelled it *la ñapa*. The Creoles changed the spelling to the more French sounding lagniappe.

From Mark Twain in <u>Life on the Mississippi</u>:
"We picked up one excellent word--a word worth traveling to New Orleans to get; a nice limber, expressive, handy word--'lagniappe.'. . . It is the equivalent of the thirteenth roll in a 'baker's dozen.' It is something thrown in, gratis, for good measure."

Cajun and Creole Seasonings

Ready to use seasoning mixes can add a lot to your cooking. You can buy them on the internet if you can't find them at your local grocer. Or, you can make a large batch of your own. As long as you keep it in an airtight container it will last for a really long time.

Just like with gumbo, you can make these spice mixes your way. Just add a little more or a little less of whatever you like or don't like.

 *Think about making a huge batch. A jar of your own Cajun or Creole seasoning makes a great gift for family and friends.*

Cajun Seasoning Mix

26 ounces of table salt
5 Tablespoons cayenne pepper
3 Tablespoons black pepper
3 Tablespoons onion powder
3 Tablespoons garlic powder
3 Tablespoons chili powder
1 Tablespoon dried basil flakes.
1 Tablespoon bay leaf powder

Mix all ingredients well in a large bowl and then transfer to glass jars with tight tops. If you have an 8 cup measuring cup it'll work better for the transfer because of the spout.

Note: *bay leaf powder is hard to find. If you can't find it, slip several whole dried bay leaves into each jar. The fragrance of the bay will be infused into the rest of the mix. And, if you are giving the jars as gifts, it looks good.*

Creole Seasoning Mix I

2 tablespoons paprika
2 tablespoons salt
2 tablespoons garlic powder
1 tablespoon black pepper
1 tablespoon onion powder
1 tablespoon cayenne pepper
1 tablespoon dried oregano
1 tablespoon dried thyme

Mix all ingredients well and transfer to a glass jar with a tight top

Creole Seasoning Mix II

2 tablespoons onion powder
2 tablespoons garlic powder
2 tablespoons dried oregano leaves
2 tablespoons dried basil

1 tablespoon dried thyme leaves
1 tablespoon black pepper
1 tablespoon white pepper
1 tablespoon cayenne pepper
1 tablespoon celery seed
5 tablespoons paprika

Mix all ingredients well and transfer to a glass jar with a tight top

Easy Shrimp and Corn Chowder

1 stick butter
1 medium onion, chopped
1 bell pepper, chopped
2 seafood bouillon cubes
2 cans of creamed corn
4 cans cream of potato soup
1 quart of milk
2 teaspoons Creole seasoning
Salt and pepper to taste
1 pound frozen peeled shrimp or crawfish tails
1 bunch of green onions, chopped

Melt the butter in a large soup pot and sauté the onion and bell pepper until tender. Add the remaining ingredients except the shrimp or crawfish and green onions.

Simmer this mixture for about 15 minutes stirring often. If it's too thick add a little more milk. Add the shrimp or crawfish and green onions and simmer for 10 more minutes.

Serves 6-8.

Crawfish and Corn Chowder

12 ounces bacon
2 cups diced potatoes
1 medium onion, chopped
2 16 ounce cans of creamed corn
2 pints half and half
2 teaspoons butter
1 teaspoon Creole seasoning
1 teaspoon Tabasco sauce or to taste
1 pound peeled crawfish tails

Fry bacon until crisp. Discard all but enough of the bacon grease for you to sauté the potatoes and onions. Sauté them for about 15 minutes.

Add butter, corn, half and half, seasoning and Tabasco. Crumble the bacon and add it to the chowder. Simmer for 25 to 30 minutes or until the potatoes are fork tender.

Add the crawfish and continue to simmer 15 minutes. If the chowder is too thick, add a little warm milk.

Serves 6.

Oyster and Spinach Chowder

There are so many ways to make this your own. Add cooked, diced potatoes, shredded carrots, garlic, parsley, Tabasco. Use butter instead of olive oil and save some of the cheese to sprinkle on top while serving.

3 tablespoons olive oil
1/2 cup flour
1 medium onion, chopped
1/2 cup chopped green onions
1 cup sliced fresh mushrooms
1 bag of fresh baby spinach leaves, torn if large
2 cups chicken broth or clam juice
5 cups milk
3 pints whole oysters
1 cup shredded Cheddar cheese
Salt and pepper to taste

In a large heavy pot combine the flour and oil to make your roux. Cook on a medium high heat, stirring constantly for just about 4 minutes. Remember, this is not gumbo! You are making a white roux.

Add the onion and mushrooms. Cook, stirring constantly until they're tender. Add the spinach, a bit at a time and then the green onion. Cook just until the spinach is wilted.

Pour the broth and milk into the pot slowly while stirring. Let the soup simmer for about 10 minutes while you pick through the oysters with your cleaned hands for shells. Drain the oysters into a bowl. If the soup is too thick you'll need this liquid to thin it out.

Add the oysters and cheese and cook while stirring just until the cheese has melted. Add salt and pepper to taste and serve immediately.

Serves 8.

Notes:

_____

_____

_____

_____

New England Clam or Oyster Chowder

8 slices of bacon, diced
1 1/2 medium onions, chopped
2 stalks celery, diced
3 tablespoons flour
2 cups clam juice
2 cups whole milk
1 cup heavy cream
1 pound of small Yukon Gold potatoes, peeled
  and diced
1 tablespoon chopped fresh thyme
1 can of corn kernels
1 bay leaf
Cayenne pepper to taste
1 dash Worcestershire sauce
1/2 teaspoon Old Bay seasoning
40 littleneck clams or 25 oysters, shucked
  and chopped
Salt and pepper to taste

In a large heavy pot, cook the bacon until right
before it's crisp. Add the onions and celery and
sauté in the bacon fat until they are tender but
not brown. Sprinkle the flour in and cook
stirring constantly for about 4 minutes. You are
making a white roux, not a brown one.

Add the clam juice, milk and cream slowly and
stir well to blend with the flour. Add the potatoes

and thyme and allow to simmer for 10 minutes or until the potatoes are almost fork tender.

Put in the corn, bay leaf and other seasonings and simmer for another 5-10 minutes. Check the potatoes to make sure they're fully cooked.

Add the clams or oysters and cook for 5 more minutes. You don't want to overcook them.

Serves 8.

Notes:

_____

_____

_____

_____

_____

Red Bean Soup

2 cups red dried kidney beans
1/2 pound raw bacon
1/4 cup olive oil
1 large onion, chopped
1 bell pepper, chopped
2 celery stalks, chopped
1 teaspoon cumin, optional
Cayenne pepper to taste
Salt to taste
6 cups water
3 bay leaves
1/3 cup chopped green onions

If you are using dried beans, soak them overnight. If you are using canned kidney beans, you can cut the cooking time in half.

In a large heavy pot cook the bacon until it's crisp. Remove the bacon and pour off the excess fat from the pot. When the bacon is cool enough, crumble it.

Add the olive oil to the pot and sauté the onion, bell pepper and celery until they are soft but not browned.

Add the cumin, salt, pepper, bacon, water and bay leaves. Simmer for 2 hours or until the beans are tender.

When the beans are soft, remove about half of them from the pot to a bowl. Using a fork, mash them well and then return them to the pot and stir well. This will give you a thick, rich soup.

Serve over white rice to 8 hungry people.

Candied Yams

Let's get some things straight first. A yam is not a sweet potato and a sweet potato is not a potato at all! A yam is actually a brown tuber with a bark like covering that can grow up to 4 ½ feet long. They are rarely found in this country. The sweet potato was domesticated in Central and South America thousands of years ago. The yam is native to Africa and Asia.

By tradition, when they're baked I call them sweet potatoes. When they're candied I call them yams!

2 (40 ounce) cans sweet potatoes (yams),
   drained, reserve 1½ cups juice
1/2 cup brown sugar, packed
4 tablespoons butter
Cinnamon to taste
2 1/2 cups mini marshmallows

Spray a 13x9 casserole dish with cooking spray. Arrange the drained sweet potatoes in the dish.

Melt the butter with the sugar in a saucepan while stirring. Remove the saucepan from the stove and stir in the juice from the cans and the cinnamon blending well.

Pour this mixture over sweet potatoes in the dish.

Bake at 350° for about 45 minutes. Remove the dish from the oven and sprinkle it generously with the marshmallows. Return the dish to the oven and bake just until the marshmallows begin to brown. Be careful not to burn them!

Bread Pudding
With Bourbon Sauce

1 loaf stale French bread, cubed into 1-inch
   squares (about 6 or 7 cups)
1 quart whole milk
3 large eggs
2 cups sugar (white or light brown)
2 tablespoons vanilla extract
1/4 teaspoon nutmeg
1/2 teaspoon cinnamon
3 tablespoons butter, melted

Bourbon Sauce

1 cup packed brown sugar
1 stick butter
2 tablespoons whipping cream
1/3 cup of bourbon

Preheat oven to 350° and use the melted butter to grease sides and bottom of a 9"x13" baking pan.

Place the bread cubes into a large bowl. Pour the milk over it and then, using your cleaned hands, mash it down until all of the milk is absorbed.

In a separate bowl, whisk the eggs, sugar, vanilla, nutmeg and cinnamon together. Pour this over the bread and milk mixture. Add the raisins and stir gently until it is well mixed.

Pour the bread, milk and egg mixture into the baking pan. Bake at 350°F for 35-45 minutes, until it looks set. The pudding is done when the edges start getting light brown and start to pull away from the edge of the pan.

To make the bourbon sauce: Put all of the sauce ingredients into a heavy saucepan, stirring constantly, until the mixture comes to a boil and the sugar is completely dissolved. It's ready to serve over your warm bread pudding.

Variations:

Adults only? Soak raisins in bourbon and put them into the pudding mixture before baking.

Children? The quickest ever sauce – pour a small box of instant vanilla pudding into a small bowl. Start pouring milk into it while whisking. Add more milk until it is the right consistency.

Like it fruitier? Drain a can of fruit cocktail and add it. Or dice drained canned peaches. Or . . .

You've got a serious sweet tooth? Instead of bread use leftover donuts. If they're glazed donuts, omit about half of the sugar from the recipe.

Try substituting stale croissants for the bread. Yum!

Notes:

_____

_____

_____

_____

_____

Creamy New Orleans Pralines

1 cup light brown sugar, packed
1/2 cup granulated sugar
1/2 cup whipping cream
4 tablespoons butter
2 tablespoons water
1 teaspoon vanilla
1 cup pecan halves

Make sure you have all of your ingredients lined up and ready to go and your pan lined with wax paper or parchment. To get a perfect praline, many of these steps have to be done quickly. Also, it's important to remember that pralines should be made on a dry, low humidity day.

In a heavy-bottomed 2 quart saucepan, combine all of the ingredients except the vanilla and pecans.

On medium high heat bring the mixture to a gentle boil to melt the sugar, stirring constantly with a wooden spatula. Be sure to incorporate any sugar that is clinging to sides of the pot.

Cook this mixture until it reaches the soft ball stage or 238° on a candy thermometer. Remove the pan from the stove and add the vanilla and pecans.

Stir vigorously for about a minute or two until the pecans are suspended in the mixture but the whole thing is still glossy.

Drop the pralines quickly before the mixture cools in large spoonsful onto your lined pans. Be careful because the praline mixture is still very hot.

Did you overcook them or wait too long to spoon out the mixture? Pralines too hard? Not a problem *– crumble them up and sprinkle them on top of vanilla ice cream, top a cheesecake, incorporate them into brownies, etc. Delicious! Put extra crumbles in an airtight jar and into your refrigerator where they will keep for several weeks. You probably will have eaten them before those weeks are up!*

If your pralines are too soft, refrigerate them until they're a little harder and then roll them into balls. Dip them into melted candy making chocolate and call them truffles.

Note: *A sure giveaway as to whether or not you're from the Gulf Coast is how you pronounce pralines and pecans. In this area they are always called "praw-leens" and "pi-cawns".*

Sources and Resources

Looking for **The Perfect Gumbo Spoon®?**

Email us at info@perfectspoons.com and we'll tell you who sells them near you. Retailers can find us at www.perfectspoons.com

You can find also find them online at FrenchQuarterMarket.com, CarolineAndCo.com, Amazon.com, PiecesofEightGifts.com and other fine online sellers.

Looking for really great 16 ounce **gumbo bowls**? Check this great one out at FrenchQuarterMarket.com.

Can't find the **Cajun and Creole seasonings**, sauces, instant roux and other mixes? JandSFoods.com has a great selection and great prices.

About the Author

 I grew up in Baton Rouge, Louisiana, a city that's west of Creole country and east of Cajun county. There's a lot of talk these days about the new fusion foods, the culinary blending of cultures. In Baton Rouge we've had fusion foods for hundreds of years!

When I was 19, I took off for Paris where, among other fun pursuits, I studied French cooking. Since then I've managed to travel to and, of course, eat in most of Europe, Asia, Africa and Central America. Did I take cooking classes in those places? No! By then I had already learned that overall the best food was to be found in South Louisiana.

Some years ago when the Sugarbusters! diet was at its height of popularity I wrote three different cookbooks that could be used with the diet. I was delighted at how well they were received but I knew even then that one day I would have to write about gumbo.

My parents were both masterful cooks and preparing family meals was a labor of love. I really believe that it's that love and passion for good food, along with our plentiful and sometimes unique ingredients, that have fused to make Creole and Cajun cooking renowned across the world. Our quintessential dish? Of course it's gumbo!

Notes:

_____

_____

_____

_____

_____

_____

_____

_____

_____

_____

_____

_____

_____

_____

_____

Notes:

_____

_____

_____

_____

_____

_____

_____

_____

_____

_____

_____

_____

_____

_____

_____

_____